Fortune Cards

Tarot & Zodiac Coloring Book

Gothic Occult Astrology Cards

For Adults & Teens

Rachel Mintz

THE DEVIL

♑ Capricorn

♉ Taurus

Cancer

Aries

Pisces

Scorpio

Virgo

Sagittarius

Aquarius

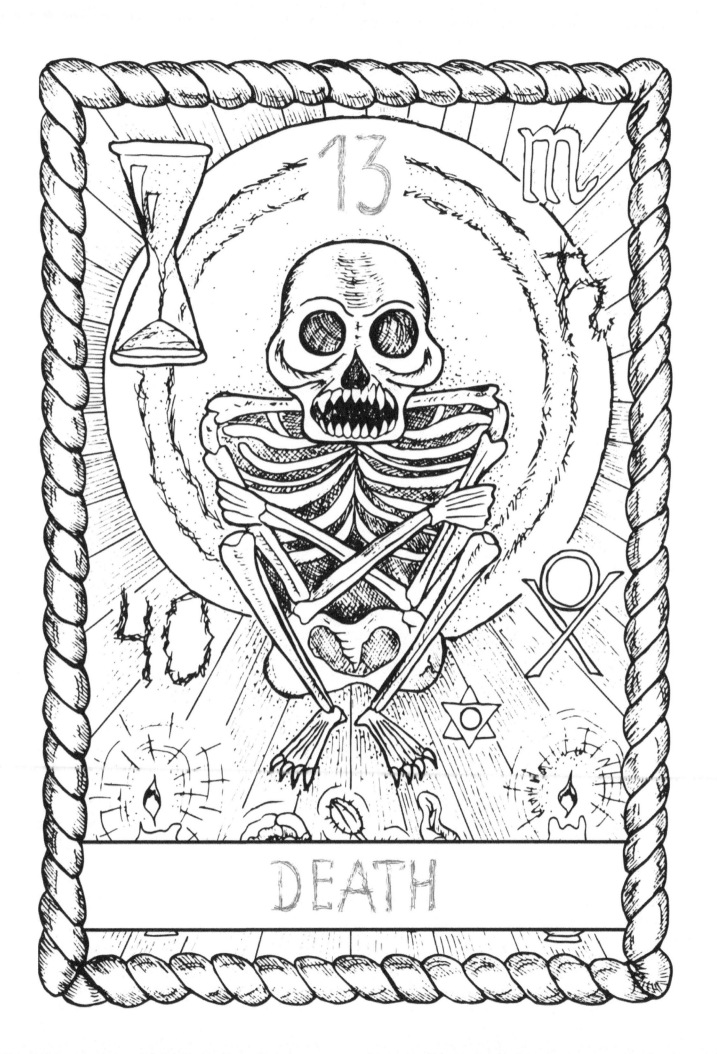

DEATH

THE TOWER

THE MAGICIAN

THE LOVERS

THE WORLD

THE HIGH PRIESTESS

ACE OF CUPS

WHEEL OF FORTUNE

XIX

THE SUN.

XII

THE HANGED MAN.

JUDGEMENT.

THE TOWER.

THE FOOL.

Thank you for coloring with us

Please rate & review

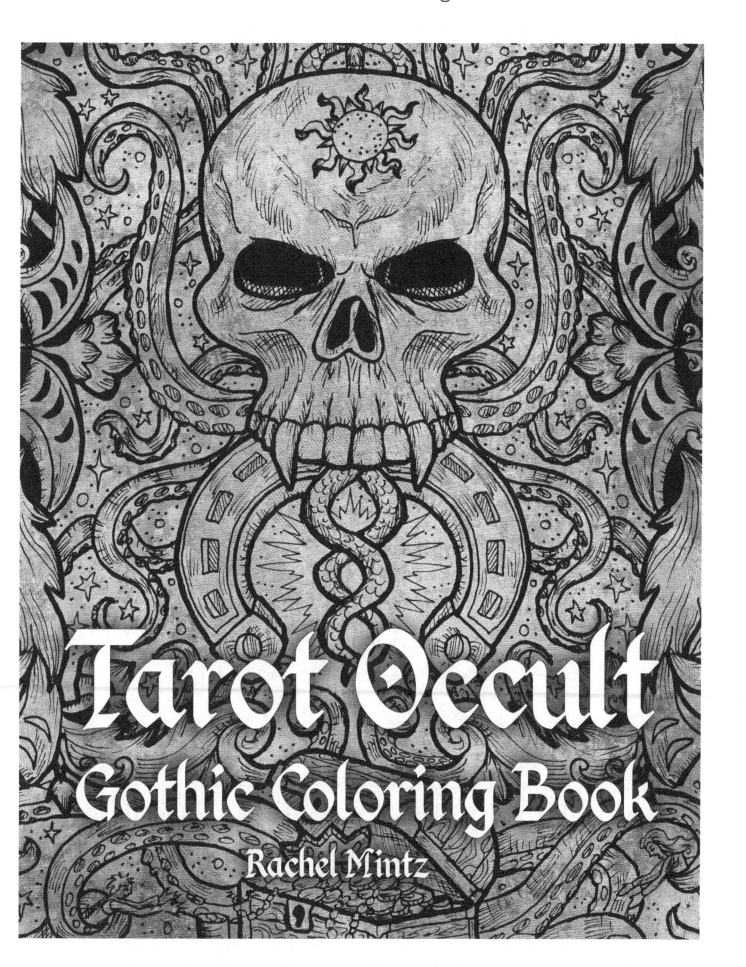

Tarot Occult

Gothic Coloring Book

Rachel Mintz

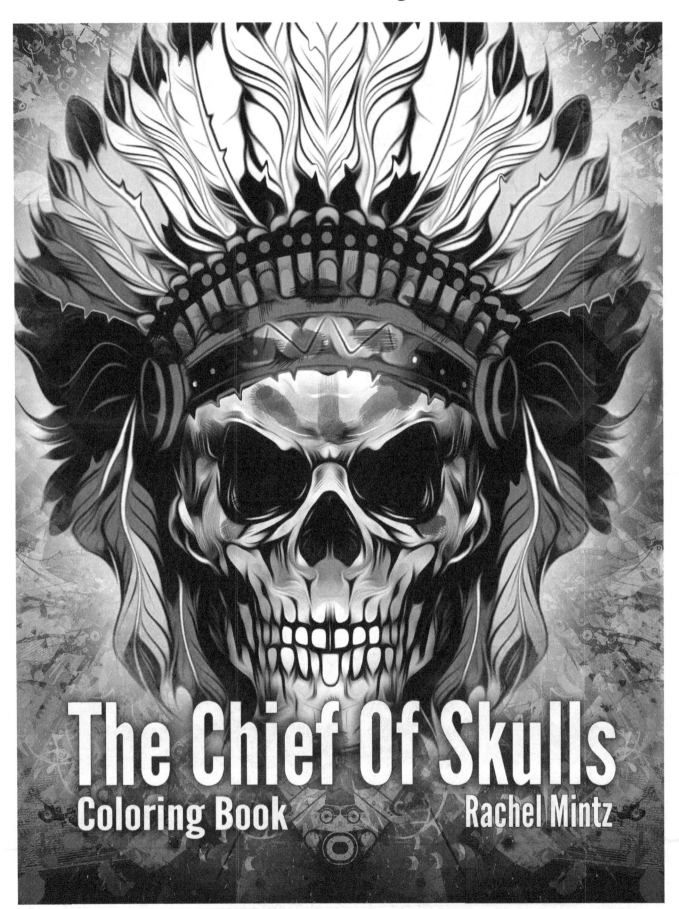

The Chief Of Skulls
Coloring Book   Rachel Mintz

Look for more RACHEL MINTZ coloring books at Amazon.

Mandalas | Wildlife | Marine Life| **Portraits** | Dogs | Cats | **Flowers** | Skulls | Gothic | Architecture | Romantic | Texts & Sayings | Ethnic | Steampunk | **Fashion** | Horses | Unicorns | Witches | Horror | Grayscale | Sports | Christmas | Holidays | Kids | Cars | **Motorbikes** | Trucks | Urban | Fairies | **Jewish Holidays**: Passover, Hanukkah, Purim | Safari | Pets |Multicultural | Educational for Kids | Back to School | **Preschool & Toddlers** | Army & Military | Knights & Castles | Dragons | Princesses | Butterflies | Birds | Reptiles | Bible | **Stained Glass** | Abstract | Machines | **Robots** | Space & Science | **Zombies** | Monsters | And many more topics..

Which topic do you like to color?

Search Amazon for 'Rachel Mintz + Your Topic' and find a book to color or as a gift.

Thank you for coloring with us

We will be very thankful if you could take the time to rate & review this book

Made in the USA
Las Vegas, NV
11 February 2024